# ONE-PAGE
# MATH GAMES

## 30 Super-Easy, Super-Fun Reproducible Games for Seatwork, Centers, Homework, and More!

**Lory Evans**

New York • Toronto • London • Auckland • Sydney
Mexico City • New Delhi • Hong Kong • Buenos Aires

**Teaching** *Resources*

# DEDICATION

To my parents who provided me with the education and encouragement to live my professional dream

To my husband and children who allow me to be Mrs. Evans during the daytime—I love you with all my heart

To my Creekside Elementary friends who make my daily duties a delight

Editor: Mela Ottaiano
Cover design: Jason Robinson
Interior design: Keka Interactive
Cover and interior illustrations: Teresa Anderko

ISBN: 978-0-545-31475-6

3 4 5 6 7 8 9 10    40    17 16 15 14 13 12 11

# Contents

INTRODUCTION ........................................................... 5

ONE-PAGE MATH GAMES

1 **Out in Space**
   Skill: Number Sense ........................................................ 10

2 **Clowning Around**
   Skill: Number Sense ........................................................ 11

3 **Off the Board**
   Skill: Even & Odd .......................................................... 12

4 **Headin' Home**
   Skill: Even & Odd .......................................................... 13

5 **Goal!**
   Skill: Place Value ......................................................... 14

6 **Hundreds of Horses**
   Skill: Place Value ......................................................... 15

7 **E.I.E.I.O.**
   Skill: Addition ............................................................ 16

8 **Dinosaur Dots**
   Skill: Addition ............................................................ 17

9 **Shuttle Subtraction**
   Skill: Subtraction ......................................................... 18

10 **Spot a Spider**
    Skill: Subtraction ........................................................ 19

11 **Tick Tock**
    Skill: Time ............................................................... 20

12 **Tick Tock Tac Toe**
    Skill: Time ............................................................... 21

13 **Spin Your Wheels**
    Skill: Money .............................................................. 22

14 **Make a Dollar**
    Skill: Money .............................................................. 23

15 **Wagon of Shapes**
    Skill: Shapes ............................................................. 24

16 **Sunny Shapes**
Skill: Shapes ............................................................................................ 25

17 **Zany Zoo**
Skill: Graphing ........................................................................................ 26

18 **Dress-Up Fun**
Skill: Graphing ........................................................................................ 27

19 **Double Dog Dare**
Skill: Doubles .......................................................................................... 28

20 **Donkey Double Plus 1**
Skill: Doubles .......................................................................................... 29

21 **Flying High**
Skills: Addition & Subtraction .................................................................. 30

22 **Racing for Raindrops**
Skills: Addition & Subtraction .................................................................. 31

23 **Itchy Insects**
Skill: Regrouping ..................................................................................... 32

24 **Lots of Spots**
Skill: Regrouping ..................................................................................... 33

25 **Skip Count Stomp: 2s & 3s**
Skill: Skip Counting ................................................................................. 34

26 **Skip Count Stomp: 5s & 10s**
Skill: Skip Counting ................................................................................. 35

27 **Blast Off!**
Skill: Multiplication .................................................................................. 36

28 **Perfect Products**
Skill: Multiplication .................................................................................. 37

29 **Feathered Fractions**
Skill: Fractions ........................................................................................ 38

30 **Fishing for Fractions**
Skill: Fractions ........................................................................................ 39

REPRODUCIBLE MANIPULATIVES ........................................................ 40

# Introduction

**W**elcome to One-Page Math Games! These 30 games target the math skills that students in grades 2–3 need to master—place value, addition, subtraction, money, and more.

I created this collection of games because I love math! It's my hope to show children that math can be fun and exciting. I also love organization and simplicity. These easy-to-prepare activities consist of one-page reproducible game boards and all use common manipulatives. The games come with clear directions that students can follow independently. They also lend themselves to many different uses. I've had the most success using them for centers and for homework.

Please enjoy the games as much as my students and I do!

*–Lory Evans*

Each skill is easy to identify.

Game materials are already in most classrooms.

Directions are simple and clear.

Game boards contain art with plenty of kid-appeal.

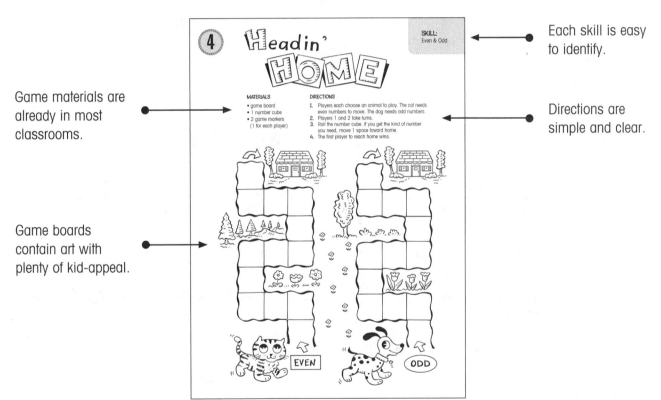

## For Centers

To manage the centers, I label a three-drawer container for supplies—transparent game markers in various colors, plastic transparent spinners, and number cubes—and use a vertical, three-tier desk organizer to house files with class sets of up to three different game boards. I begin with one game. Then each week, I introduce a new game that is applicable to our math topic, adding it to the front of the organizer. The older games rotate back one by one until students have had three weeks to play the game and master the concept. Then the game retires to my file cabinet until next year (or may appear again briefly for a quick review at the end of the year or to provide fast finishers with some meaningful skills practice.)

Each week students are invited to practice their math skills with three games, during which partners are able to discuss their problem-solving strategies, use math vocabulary, and provide additional peer support and techniques.

## For Homework

To send the games home, simply photocopy the game and relevant manipulatives. Give family members the option to use cereal, coins, or small objects as markers. When the game uses a spinner, be sure to clip a paper clip to the top of the game before sending home, and include a copy of How to Use the Spinner on page 40.

Using these games as homework is a fun way to involve family members with the curriculum. Parents and caregivers can quickly observe their child's understanding or lack of understanding and offer their support in a positive way.

## Materials

We have provided reproducible versions of many of the manipulatives called for in the games (see pages 40–48). However, you will likely have many of them on hand already. Here is a list of materials the games use:

- 1–3 number cubes
- 2–30 game markers (preferably transparent and/or in 2 different colors)
- spinner
- paper clip
- coins
- pattern blocks

## TIPS

★ To use the games over and over again, copy the games onto colorful cardstock and laminate them for durability.

★ After laminating the game, you may want to prepare a spinner by pushing a brad through the center of its space on the board. Then clip a paper clip to the game board for students to place around the brad.

★ It's best to use transparent game markers in two different colors. For games where students must remove a game marker or may replace an opponent's marker, the transparent playing pieces enable students to see the numbers on the game board. Using two different colors allows them to keep track of which pieces each student has played during the game.

★ At the beginning of each school year, consider filling several zippered plastic bags with a transparent spinner, some transparent game markers, and 2–3 number cubes that students can check out to use all year long.

## Easy Ways to Adapt the Games

Here are tips for easy ways to adapt some of the games.

**Games 1 & 2:** Use the blank 8-space spinner on page 40 to write in new numbers. For another twist, fill in the stars or balloons with numbers. Students can find a number on the board that is "less than" or "greater than" the one they spin, depending on the game.

**Games 7 & 8:** Copy the circles on page 41 (use numbers 2–12) to place different numbers over the existing numbers. You may also encourage students to roll 3 number cubes (if so, use numbers 3–18 on page 41).

**Games 9 & 10:** Copy the squares on page 40 to place different numbers over the existing numbers. Use numbers 4–9 with game 9 and numbers 2–7 with game 10.

**Games 11 & 12:** Copy the digital times on page 46 to place over the analog clocks. (In Game 11 use only times ending in ":15" or ":45.")

**Games 13:** For an extra challenge, use the blank 8-space spinner on page 40 to replace numbers 1–4 with greater numbers.

**Game 16:** Use the blank 8-space spinner on page 40 to write in different shapes. Copy the shapes on page 47 to change the grid layout.

**Game 17:** To revise the bar graph, copy the strips of different animals and/or the blank strips on page 45. Be sure to replace the squares in the player rows with the numbers 0–3 as necessary.

**Game 18:** Use the costume squares on page 45 to place over the pictures on the line graph or on the players' grids to change the game outcomes.

**Games 23 & 24:** Copy the blank squares on page 40 to place different problems over the existing addition problems.

**Games 27 & 28:** Copy the circles on page 41 to place different numbers over the existing numbers. Use only numbers 1–6, 8–10, 12, 14–16, 18, 20, 24, 25, 30, and 36.

**Games 29 & 30:** Copy the fractions or fraction representations on page 46 to place over the existing ones.

## CONNECTIONS TO MATH STANDARDS

The National Council of Teachers of Mathematics has proposed what teachers should provide for their students to become proficient in mathematics. To learn more about the NCTM standards, visit the Web site: http://standards.nctm.org. For additional information about NCTM and to learn more about the topics and benchmarks within each math standard, read Principles and Standards for School Mathematics from the National Council for Teachers of Mathematics, 2000.

The recent Common Core State Standards have also put forth guidance for what are the most important skills for students to learn at the different grade levels. To become more familiar with the math portion of these standards, visit the CCSS Web site: www.corestandards.org.

For a quick overview of how this book can support your efforts to meet math standards, see the grids on pages 8 and 9.

## Connections to the NCTM Standards

The grid below shows how the activities in this book can help meet the standards recommended by the National Council of Teachers of Mathematics.

| Activity Title | Page | Number & Operations | Algebra | Geometry | Measurement | Data Analysis & Probability | Problem Solving | Reasoning & Proof | Communication | Connections | Representation |
|---|---|---|---|---|---|---|---|---|---|---|---|
| Out In Space | 10 | ● | | | | | | | ● | | |
| Clowning Around | 11 | ● | | | | | | | ● | | |
| Off the Board | 12 | ● | | | | | | | ● | | |
| Headin' Home | 13 | ● | | | | | | | ● | | |
| Goal! | 14 | ● | | | | | | | ● | | |
| Hundreds of Horses | 15 | ● | | | | | ● | | ● | ● | |
| E.I.E.I.O. | 16 | ● | | | | | | | ● | | |
| Dinosaur Dots | 17 | ● | | | | | | | ● | | |
| Shuttle Subtraction | 18 | ● | | | | | | | ● | | |
| Spot a Spider | 19 | ● | | | | | | | ● | | |
| Tick Tock | 20 | | | | ● | | | | ● | ● | ● |
| Tick Tock Tac Toe | 21 | | | | ● | | | | ● | ● | ● |
| Spin Your Wheels | 22 | | | | ● | | | | ● | ● | |
| Make a Dollar | 23 | | | | ● | | ● | | ● | ● | |
| Wagon of Shapes | 24 | | | ● | | | | | ● | ● | |
| Sunny Shapes | 25 | | | ● | | | | | ● | ● | |
| Zany Zoo | 26 | | | | | ● | | | ● | | ● |
| Dress-Up Fun | 27 | | | | | ● | | | ● | ● | ● |
| Double Dog Dare | 28 | ● | | | | | ● | | ● | | |
| Donkey Double Plus 1 | 29 | ● | | | | | ● | | ● | | |
| Flying High | 30 | ● | | | | | ● | | ● | | |
| Racing for Raindrops | 31 | ● | | | | | | ● | ● | | |
| Itchy Insects | 32 | ● | | | | | | ● | ● | ● | |
| Lots of Spots | 33 | ● | | | | | | ● | ● | ● | |
| Skip Count Stomp: 2s & 3s | 34 | | ● | | | | | | ● | ● | |
| Skip Count Stomp: 5s & 10s | 35 | | ● | | | | | | ● | ● | |
| Blast Off! | 36 | ● | | | | | | | ● | | |
| Perfect Products | 37 | ● | | | | | | | ● | | |
| Feathered Fractions | 38 | ● | | | | | | | ● | ● | ● |
| Fishing for Fractions | 39 | ● | | | | | | | ● | ● | ● |

## Connections to the Common Core State Standards

The grid below shows how the activities in this book can help meet the standards recommended by the Common Core State Standards initiative.

| Activity Title | Page | Grade 2 Operations & Algebraic Thinking | Number & Operations in Base Ten | Measurement & Data | Geometry | Mathematical Practices | Grade 3 Operations & Algebraic Thinking | Number & Operations in Base Ten | Number & Operations—Fractions | Measurement & Data | Geometry | Mathematical Practices |
|---|---|---|---|---|---|---|---|---|---|---|---|---|
| Out In Space | 10 | | | | | ● | | | | | | ● |
| Clowning Around | 11 | | | | | ● | | | | | | ● |
| Off the Board | 12 | | | | | ● | | | | | | ● |
| Headin' Home | 13 | | | | | ● | | | | | | ● |
| Goal! | 14 | | ● | | | ● | | | | | | ● |
| Hundreds of Horses | 15 | ● | ● | | | ● | ● | ● | | | | ● |
| E.I.E.I.O. | 16 | ● | ● | | | ● | ● | | | | | ● |
| Dinosaur Dots | 17 | ● | ● | | | ● | ● | | | | | ● |
| Shuttle Subtraction | 18 | ● | ● | | | ● | ● | | | | | ● |
| Spot a Spider | 19 | ● | ● | | | ● | ● | | | | | ● |
| Tick Tock | 20 | | | ● | | ● | | | | | | ● |
| Tick Tock Tac Toe | 21 | | | ● | | ● | | | | | | ● |
| Spin Your Wheels | 22 | ● | ● | ● | | ● | | | | | | ● |
| Make a Dollar | 23 | ● | ● | ● | | ● | | | | | | ● |
| Wagon of Shapes | 24 | | | | ● | ● | | | | | ● | ● |
| Sunny Shapes | 25 | | | | ● | ● | | | | | ● | ● |
| Zany Zoo | 26 | | | ● | | ● | | | | ● | | ● |
| Dress-Up Fun | 27 | | | ● | | ● | | | | ● | | ● |
| Double Dog Dare | 28 | ● | ● | | | ● | ● | ● | | | | ● |
| Donkey Double Plus 1 | 29 | ● | ● | | | ● | ● | | | | | ● |
| Flying High | 30 | ● | ● | | | ● | ● | | | | | ● |
| Racing for Raindrops | 31 | ● | ● | | | ● | ● | ● | | | | ● |
| Itchy Insects | 32 | ● | ● | | | ● | ● | ● | | | | ● |
| Lots of Spots | 33 | ● | ● | | | ● | ● | ● | | | | ● |
| Skip Count Stomp: 2s & 3s | 34 | ● | | | | ● | ● | | | | | ● |
| Skip Count Stomp: 5s & 10s | 35 | ● | | | | ● | ● | ● | | | | ● |
| Blast Off! | 36 | | | | | ● | ● | | | | | ● |
| Perfect Products | 37 | | | | | ● | ● | | | | | ● |
| Feathered Fractions | 38 | | | | | ● | | | ● | | | ● |
| Fishing for Fractions | 39 | | | | | ● | | | ● | | | ● |

# Out in Space

## MATERIALS

- game board
- paper clip for spinner
- 10 game markers
  (5 for each player)

## DIRECTIONS

1. Each player spins the spinner.
2. The player with the smaller number places a marker on a star.
3. The first player to place 5 markers on the board wins.

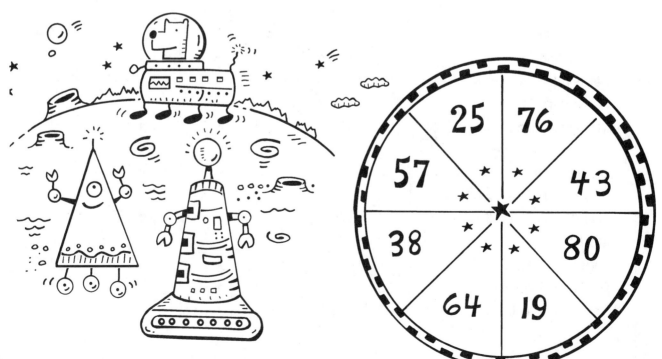

25  76
57      43
38      80
64  19

# Clowning Around

**MATERIALS**

- game board
- paper clip for spinner
- 10 game markers
  (5 for each player)

**DIRECTIONS**

1. Each player spins the spinner.
2. The player with the larger number places a marker on a balloon.
3. The first player to place 5 markers on the board wins.

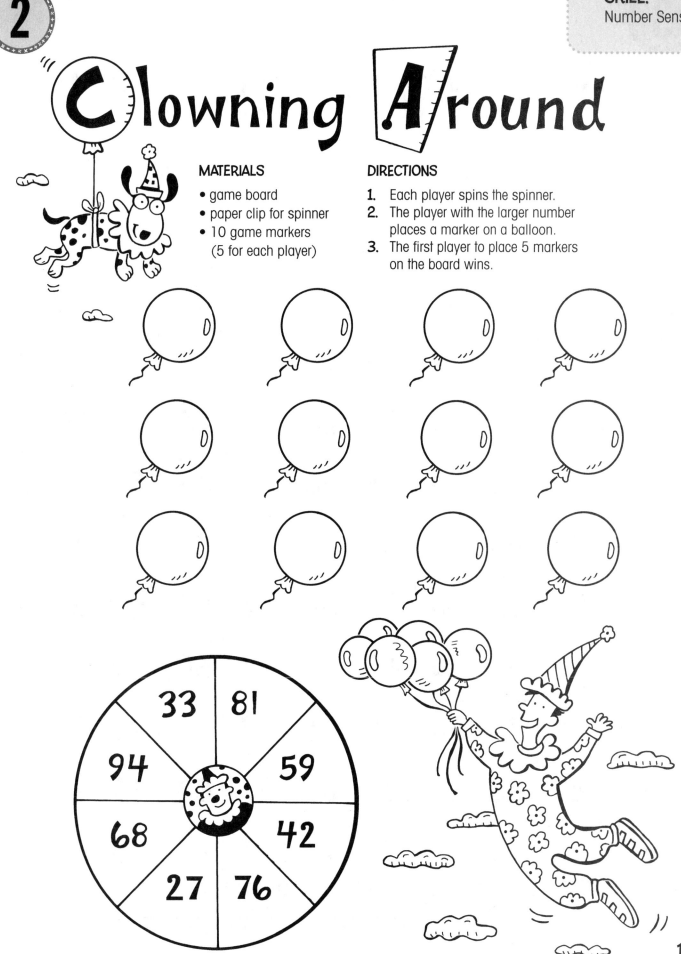

| | |
|---|---|
| 33 | 81 |
| 94 | 59 |
| 68 | 42 |
| 27 | 76 |

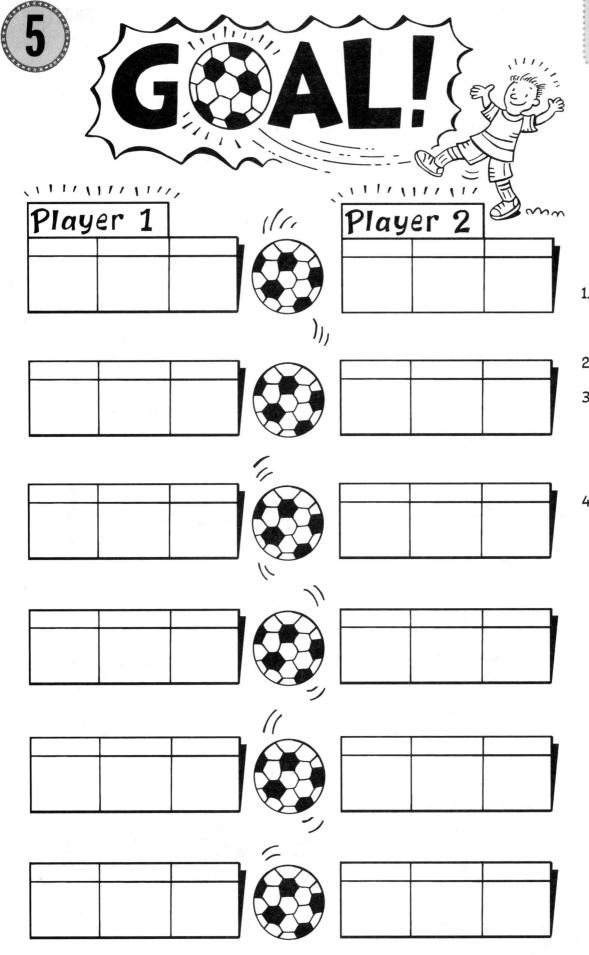

**5**

# G⚽AL!

## MATERIALS

- game board
- 3 number cubes
- 12 game markers (6 for each players)

## DIRECTIONS

1. Take turns rolling 3 number cubes to create the greatest 3-digit number.
2. Write your number on the scoreboard.
3. The player with the greatest number can place his or her marker on the soccer ball for that turn.
4. The player with the most markers on the balls at the end of the game wins.

Player 1

Player 2

# Hundreds of Horses

245

564

319

428  173

## MATERIALS

- game board
- paper clip for spinner
- 1 number cube
- 10 game markers (5 per player)

## DIRECTIONS

1. Players 1 and 2 take turns.
2. Spin the spinner to get a 3-digit number. Then roll the number cube and add that many hundreds to the 3-digit number. (For example, if you roll a 5, add 500.)
3. Find that sum on the board and cover it with a marker. If the sum is already covered, your turn is over.
4. The first player to place 3 markers in a row wins.

| | | | | |
|---|---|---|---|---|
| 419 | 1,064 | 845 | 473 | 819 |
| 273 | 245 | 964 | 428 | 345 |
| 528 | 519 | 864 | 645 | 728 |
| 545 | 628 | 673 | 319 | 764 |
| 664 | 573 | 445 | 828 | 773 |
| 919 | 928 | 619 | 664 | 745 |

# E.I.E.I.O.

## MATERIALS

- game board
- 2 number cubes
- 10 game markers
  (5 for each player)

## DIRECTIONS

1. Take turns rolling the number cubes.
2. Add the numbers together and place one marker on the answer. If the answer is already covered, your turn is over.
3. The first player to place 5 markers on the board wins.

# Dinosaur Dots

**MATERIALS**

- game board
- 2 number cubes
- 10 game markers (5 for each player)

**DIRECTIONS**

1. Take turns rolling the number cubes.
2. Add the numbers together and place one marker on the answer. If the answer is already covered, your turn is over.
3. The first player to place 5 markers on the board wins.

9

10

7

5

11

3

11

4

8

2

12

5

6

7

10

17

SKILL:
Subtraction

# SHUTTLE SUBTRACTION

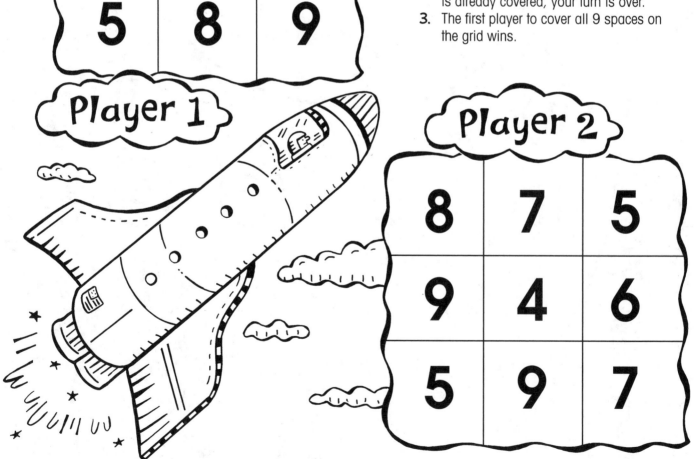

**Player 1**

| 9 | 4 | 6 |
|---|---|---|
| 6 | 7 | 8 |
| 5 | 8 | 9 |

**Player 2**

| 8 | 7 | 5 |
|---|---|---|
| 9 | 4 | 6 |
| 5 | 9 | 7 |

## MATERIALS

- game board
- 1 number cube
- 14 game markers (7 for each player)

## DIRECTIONS

1. Take turns rolling the number cube.
2. Subtract the number from 10 and place one marker on the answer. If the answer is already covered, your turn is over.
3. The first player to cover all 9 spaces on the grid wins.

One-Page Math Games © 2011 by Scholastic Inc.

# Spot a Spider

### MATERIALS

- game board
- 1 number cube
- 12 game markers
  (6 for each player)

### DIRECTIONS

1. Take turns rolling the number cube.
2. Subtract the number from 8 and place one marker on the answer. If the answer is already covered, your turn is over.
3. The first player to place 6 markers on the board wins.

Board numbers (top row): 4  7  2  5  3  6

Left column (top to bottom): 2  5  6  7  3  2

Right column (top to bottom): 4  7  5  2  3  4

Bottom row: 7  4  2  5  3  6

**13**

# Spin Your Wheels

## MATERIALS

- game board
- paper clips for spinners
- 18 game markers
  (9 for each player)

## DIRECTIONS

1. For each turn, players 1 and 2 both spin the "How Many?" and "Which Coin?" spinners to determine their coin amount.
2. The player with the greatest value covers 1 wagon wheel.
3. The first player to cover all 8 wheels wins.

## How many?

## Which coin?

**Player 1**

**Player 2**

# Make a Dollar

## MATERIALS

- game board
- paper clip for spinner
- 30 game markers
  (15 for each player)
- dollar markers

## DIRECTIONS

1. Players 1 and 2 take turns.
2. Spin the spinner and place a marker on the corresponding coin on the game board.
3. With each turn, continue to place a marker on a coin until you can add up your coins to one dollar.
4. When you make one dollar with coins, you earn a paper version to place on your wallet.
5. When all the coins are covered, the player with the most dollars on a wallet wins.

**dime** | **free choice**
**quarter** | **nickel**

Player 1

Player 2

One-Page Math Games © 2011 by Scholastic Inc.

## MATERIALS

- game board
- pattern blocks
  (1 set for each player)
- paper clip for spinner
- 8 game markers
  (4 for each player)

## DIRECTIONS

1. Players 1 and 2 take turns.
2. Spin the spinner to determine a pattern block. Place that block on one of the hexagons.
3. The player that places the block that completes a hexagon earns 1 marker to put in his or her wagon.
4. When all the hexagons are complete, the player whose wagon has the most markers wins.

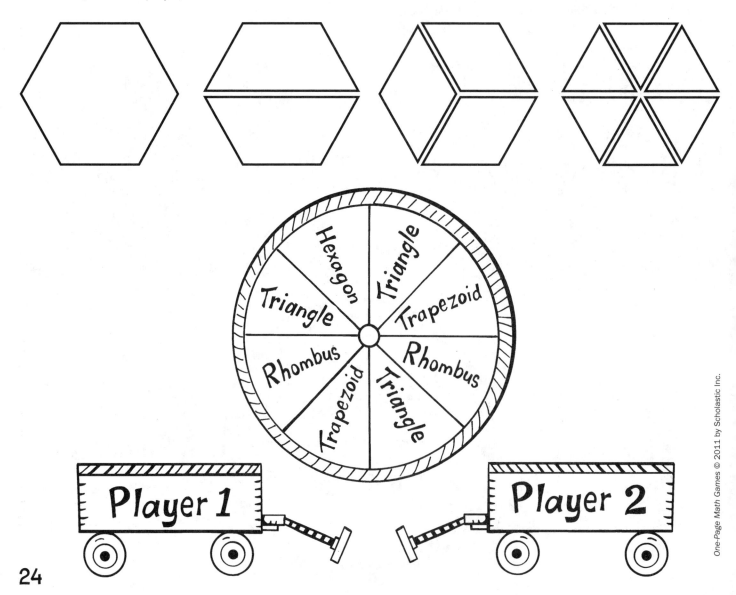

# Sunny Shapes

**Spinner shapes:** Rectangle, Trapezoid, Rhombus, Square, Triangle, Circle, Hexagon, Pentagon

## MATERIALS

- game board
- paper clip for spinner
- 24 game markers
  (12 for each player)

## DIRECTIONS

1. Players 1 and 2 take turns.
2. Spin the spinner. Place a marker on the matching shape.
3. The first player to place 5 markers in a row wins.

# Zany Zoo

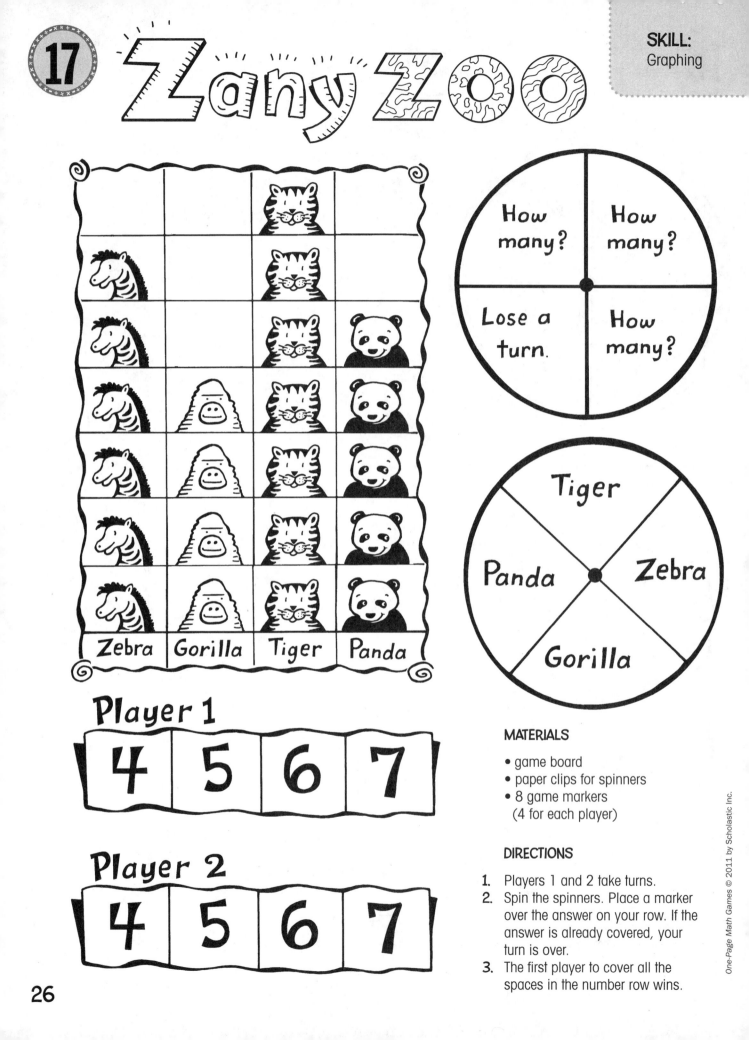

|  |  |  |  |
|---|---|---|---|
|  |  | Tiger |  |
| Zebra |  | Tiger |  |
| Zebra |  | Tiger | Panda |
| Zebra | Gorilla | Tiger | Panda |
| Zebra | Gorilla | Tiger | Panda |
| Zebra | Gorilla | Tiger | Panda |
| Zebra | Gorilla | Tiger | Panda |
| **Zebra** | **Gorilla** | **Tiger** | **Panda** |

Spinner 1: How many? / How many? / Lose a turn. / How many?

Spinner 2: Tiger / Zebra / Gorilla / Panda

## Player 1

| 4 | 5 | 6 | 7 |
|---|---|---|---|

## Player 2

| 4 | 5 | 6 | 7 |
|---|---|---|---|

### MATERIALS

- game board
- paper clips for spinners
- 8 game markers
  (4 for each player)

### DIRECTIONS

1. Players 1 and 2 take turns.
2. Spin the spinners. Place a marker over the answer on your row. If the answer is already covered, your turn is over.
3. The first player to cover all the spaces in the number row wins.

One-Page Math Games © 2011 by Scholastic Inc.

# Dress-Up Fun

## ★ Favorite Costumes ★

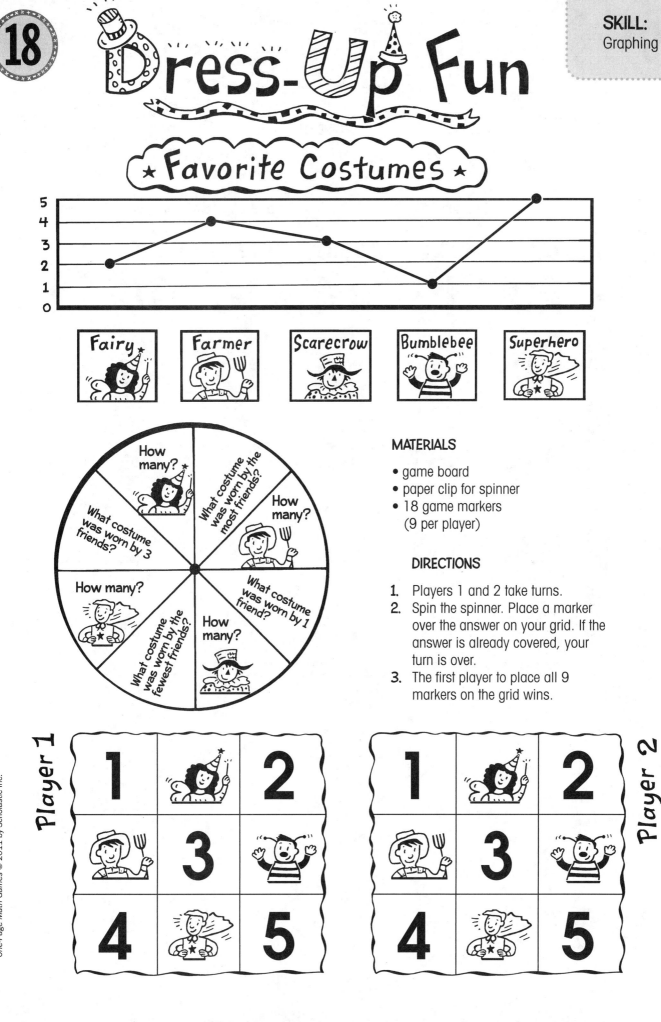

Fairy ★  Farmer  Scarecrow  Bumblebee  Superhero

### MATERIALS

- game board
- paper clip for spinner
- 18 game markers
  (9 per player)

### DIRECTIONS

1. Players 1 and 2 take turns.
2. Spin the spinner. Place a marker over the answer on your grid. If the answer is already covered, your turn is over.
3. The first player to place all 9 markers on the grid wins.

Player 1

| 1 | | 2 |
|---|---|---|
| | 3 | |
| 4 | | 5 |

Player 2

| 1 | | 2 |
|---|---|---|
| | 3 | |
| 4 | | 5 |

27

# Double Dog Dare

## MATERIALS

- game board
- paper clip for spinner
- 16 game markers
  (8 for each player)

## DIRECTIONS

1. Players 1 and 2 take turns.
2. Spin the spinner. Double the number and place a marker on one right answer.
3. The first player to place 3 markers in a row wins.

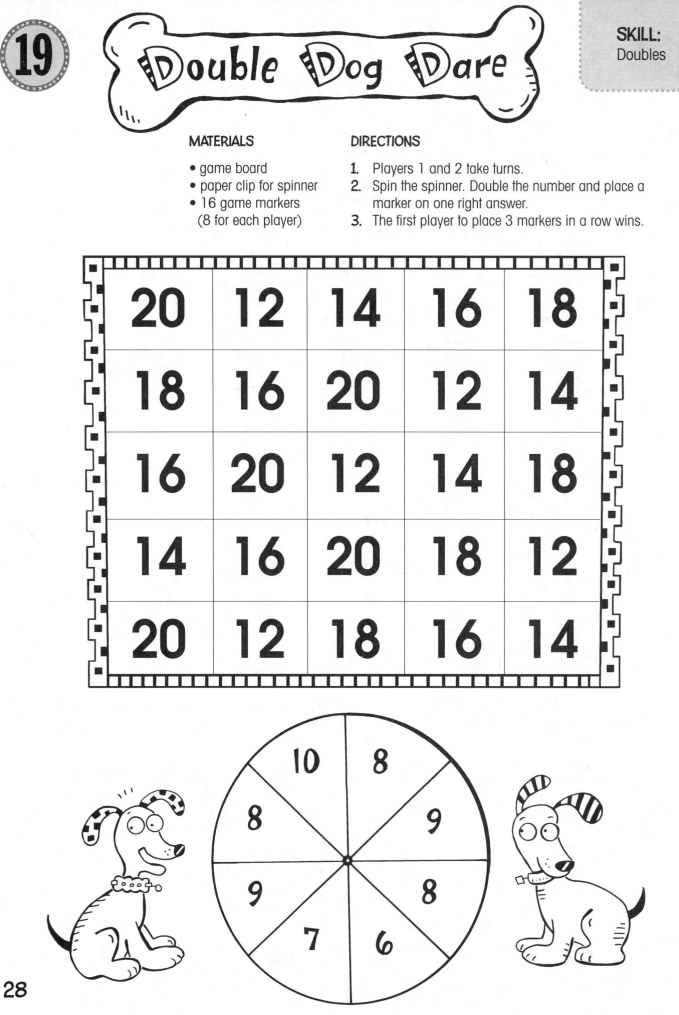

| 20 | 12 | 14 | 16 | 18 |
| 18 | 16 | 20 | 12 | 14 |
| 16 | 20 | 12 | 14 | 18 |
| 14 | 16 | 20 | 18 | 12 |
| 20 | 12 | 18 | 16 | 14 |

Spinner: 10  8  8  9  9  8  7  6

**20**

# Donkey Double Plus 1

## MATERIALS

- game board
- 1 number cube
- 16 game markers
  (8 for each player)

## DIRECTIONS

1. Players 1 and 2 take turns.
2. Roll the number cube. Double the number and add 1. Place a marker on one right answer. If your opponent already has a marker on that number you may take it off and put down your own marker.
3. The first player to place 3 markers in a row wins.

| 9 | 7 | 5 | 3 | 9 |
|---|---|---|---|---|
| 5 | 11 | 13 | 7 | 5 |
| 11 | 9 | 13 | 9 | 3 |
| 7 | 3 | 5 | 11 | 13 |
| 13 | 11 | 7 | 9 | 5 |
| 9 | 3 | 13 | 11 | 7 |

Flying High

SKILLS:
Addition &
Subtraction

**MATERIALS**

- game board
- 2 number cubes
- 24 game markers (12 for each player)

**DIRECTIONS**

1. Place markers on numbers 1–12 fo each pilot.
2. Pilots 1 and 2 take turns.
3. Roll the number cubes. Add or subtract the numbers. Then remove the marker covering the answer.
4. The first pilot to clear the board wins.

Pilot 1 ☆ ☆ ☆ ☆ ☆

| 1 | 2 | 3 | 4 | 5 | 6 |
|---|---|---|---|---|---|
| 7 | 8 | 9 | 10 | 11 | 12 |

Pilot 2 ☆ ☆ ☆ ☆ ☆

| 1 | 2 | 3 | 4 | 5 | 6 |
|---|---|---|---|---|---|
| 7 | 8 | 9 | 10 | 11 | 12 |

SKILLS:
Addition &
Subtraction

# Racing for Raindrops

17  11  8  13

16  14  6  12

18  10  7  9

15  17  8  16

## MATERIALS

- game board
- 2 number cubes
- 14 game markers
  (7 for each player)

## DIRECTIONS

1. Players 1 and 2 take turns.
2. Roll the number cubes. Add the numbers together.
3. Next, subtract that sum from 20 and place a marker on one right answer. If the answer is already covered, your turn is over.
4. The first player to place 7 markers on the board wins.

## 23  tchy Insects

**MATERIALS**

- game board
- paper clip for spinner
- 10 game markers
  (5 for each player)

**DIRECTIONS**

1. Players 1 and 2 take turns.
2. Spin the spinner. Place a marker on that kind of number sentence on the game board. If the number sentence is not available, your turn is over.
3. The first player to place 5 markers on the board wins.

| | | | | |
|---|---|---|---|---|
| 29<br>+ 29 | 18<br>+ 17 | 33<br>+ 12 | 44<br>+ 27 | 13<br>+ 14 |
| 66<br>+ 27 | 35<br>+ 21 | 72<br>+ 42 | 58<br>+ 15 | 80<br>+ 9 |
| 38<br>+ 32 | 41<br>+ 38 | 64<br>+ 17 | 22<br>+ 28 | 13<br>+ 25 |
| 54<br>+ 34 | 77<br>+ 24 | 31<br>+ 49 | 57<br>+ 45 | 91<br>+ 4 |
| | 62<br>+ 28 | 44<br>+ 16 | 73<br>+ 49 | 84<br>+ 17 |

Spinner: **Need to regroup** / **No regrouping** / **No regrouping** / **Need to regroup**

# Lots of Spots

SKILL:
Regrouping

## MATERIALS

- game board
- paper clip for spinner
- 12 game markers
  (6 for each player)

## DIRECTIONS

1. Players 1 and 2 take turns.
2. Spin the spinner to determine the answer.
   Place a marker on the number sentence on
   the game board that goes with the answer.
   If the number sentence is not available, your
   turn is over.
3. The first player to place 6 markers on the
   board wins.

| | | | |
|---|---|---|---|
| 18<br>+ 9 | 27<br>+ 27 | 36<br>+ 27 | 24<br>+ 24 |
| 14<br>+ 13 | 37<br>+ 17 | 44<br>+ 19 | 29<br>+ 19 | 32<br>+ 16 |
| 17<br>+ 46 | 19<br>+ 35 | 17<br>+ 10 | 34<br>+ 20 | 29<br>+ 34 |
| 21<br>+ 42 | 33<br>+ 15 | 39<br>+ 9 | 42<br>+ 12 | 11<br>+ 16 |
| 19<br>+ 8 | 53<br>+ 10 | 27<br>+ 21 | 12<br>+ 15 | 26<br>+ 28 |

Spinner: 27, 63, 48, 54

# Skip Count Stomp

| 6 | 10 | 4 |
|---|----|---|
| 2 | 8 | 12 |
| 4 | 6 | 10 |

← 2s

3s →

| 9 | 15 | 6 |
|----|----|---|
| 18 | 3 | 12 |
| 6 | 15 | 9 |

**MATERIALS**

- game board
- 1 number cube
- 18 transparent game markers (9 for each player)

**DIRECTIONS**

1. Each player covers the spaces on his or her board with markers.
2. Players 1 and 2 take turns.
3. Roll the number cube to find out how many times you should skip count. Then, skip count by 2s or 3s. Take a marker off the number you skip count to. If the marker has already been removed, your turn is over.
4. The first player to remove all the markers wins.

**26**

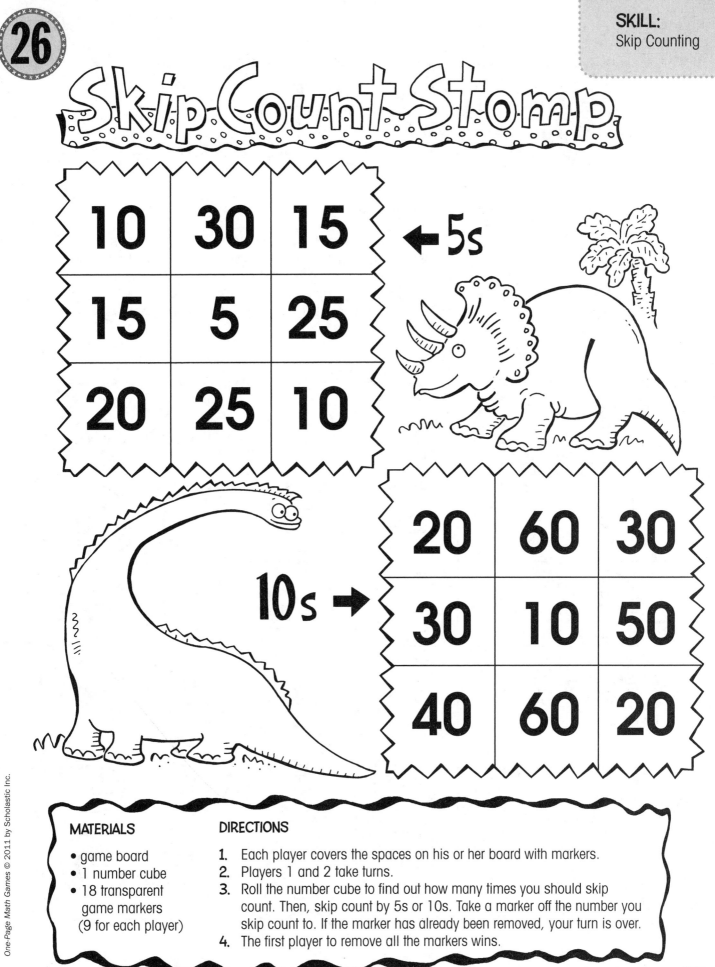

# Skip Count Stomp

**SKILL:**
Skip Counting

← 5s

| | | |
|---|---|---|
| 10 | 30 | 15 |
| 15 | 5 | 25 |
| 20 | 25 | 10 |

10s →

| | | |
|---|---|---|
| 20 | 60 | 30 |
| 30 | 10 | 50 |
| 40 | 60 | 20 |

**MATERIALS**

- game board
- 1 number cube
- 18 transparent game markers (9 for each player)

**DIRECTIONS**

1. Each player covers the spaces on his or her board with markers.
2. Players 1 and 2 take turns.
3. Roll the number cube to find out how many times you should skip count. Then, skip count by 5s or 10s. Take a marker off the number you skip count to. If the marker has already been removed, your turn is over.
4. The first player to remove all the markers wins.

One-Page Math Games © 2011 by Scholastic Inc.

# BLAST OFF!

**MATERIALS**

- game board
- 2 number cubes
- 16 game markers
  (8 for each player)

**DIRECTIONS**

1. Players 1 and 2 take turns.
2. Roll the number cubes. Multiply the numbers and place a marker on the product. If the other player already has a marker on that number, you may take it off and put down your own.
3. The first player to place 3 markers in a row wins.

| | | | | | |
|---|---|---|---|---|---|
| 6 | 3 | 10 | 5 | 20 | 24 |
| 9 | 10 | 24 | 20 | 2 | 15 |
| 2 | 16 | 1 | 15 | 8 | 6 |
| 36 | 8 | 16 | 4 | 12 | 18 |
| 4 | 12 | 20 | 5 | 16 | 25 |
| 1 | 25 | 18 | 24 | 30 | 10 |

# Perfect Products

**SKILL:**
Multiplication

**MATERIALS**

- game board
- 2 number cubes
- 12 game markers
  (6 for each player)

## DIRECTIONS

1. Players 1 and 2 take turns.
2. Roll the number cubes. Multiply the numbers and place a marker on the product. If the other player already has a marker on that number, you may take it off and put down your own marker.
3. The first player to place 6 markers on the board wins.

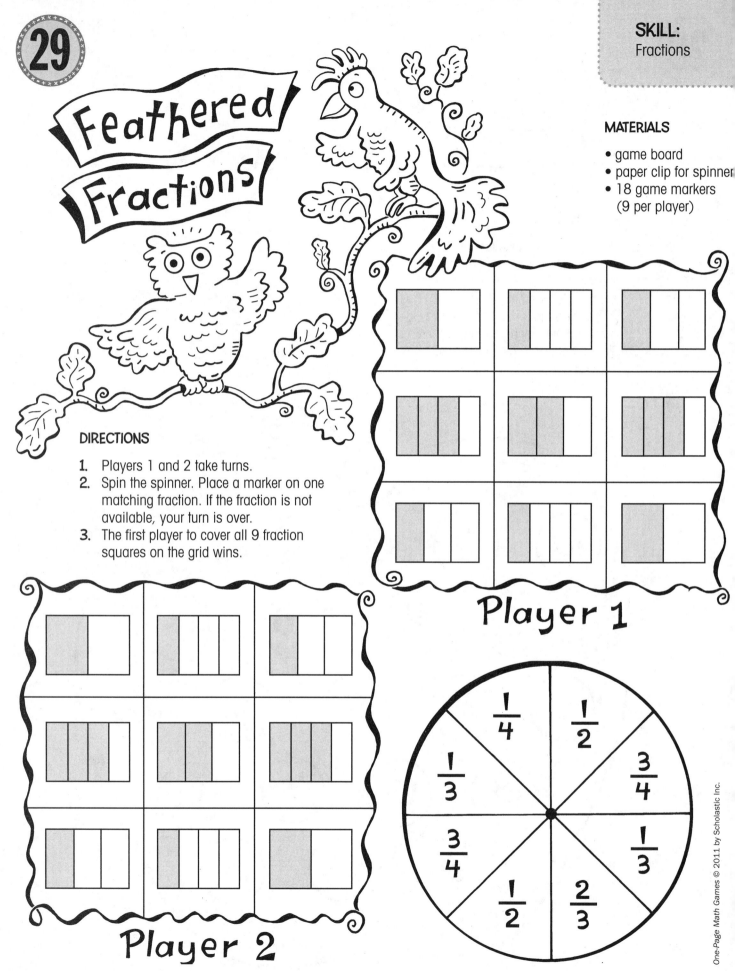

**29**

# Feathered Fractions

**SKILL:**
Fractions

**MATERIALS**

- game board
- paper clip for spinner
- 18 game markers
  (9 per player)

## DIRECTIONS

1. Players 1 and 2 take turns.
2. Spin the spinner. Place a marker on one matching fraction. If the fraction is not available, your turn is over.
3. The first player to cover all 9 fraction squares on the grid wins.

**Player 1**

**Player 2**

$\frac{1}{4}$  $\frac{1}{2}$  $\frac{3}{4}$  $\frac{1}{3}$  $\frac{2}{3}$  $\frac{1}{2}$  $\frac{3}{4}$  $\frac{1}{3}$

One-Page Math Games © 2011 by Scholastic Inc.

38

# "Fishing for Fractions

## MATERIALS

- game board
- paper clip for spinner
- 20 game markers
  (10 for each player)

## DIRECTIONS

1. Players 1 and 2 take turns.
2. Spin the spinner. Place a marker on one matching fraction. If the fraction is not available, your turn is over.
3. The first player to cover all 10 fraction squares on the grid wins.

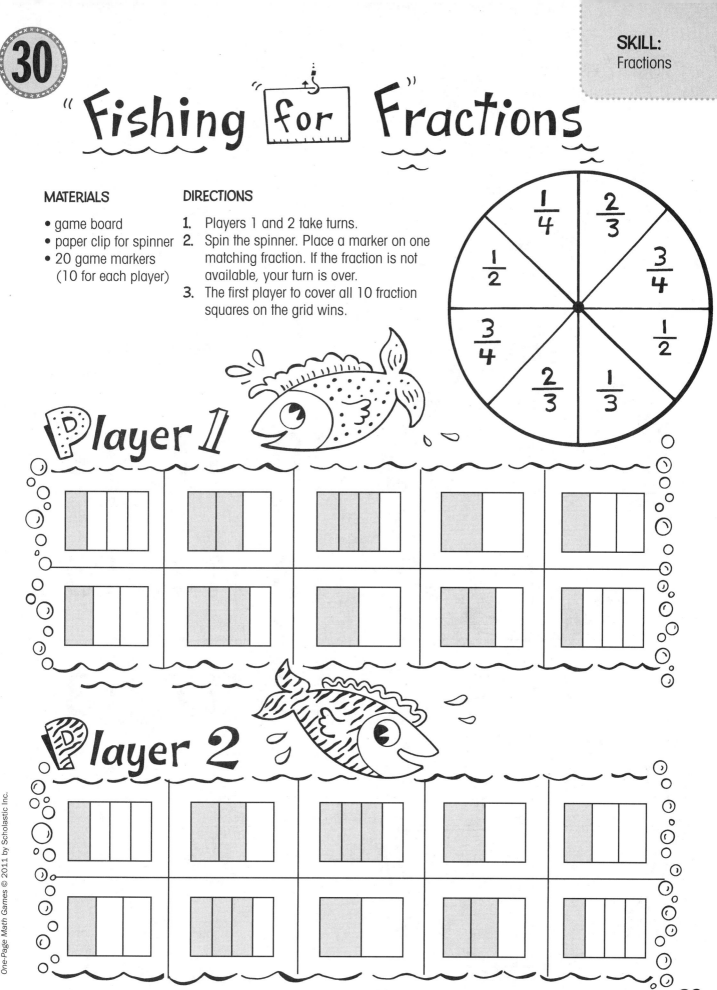

## Player 1

## Player 2

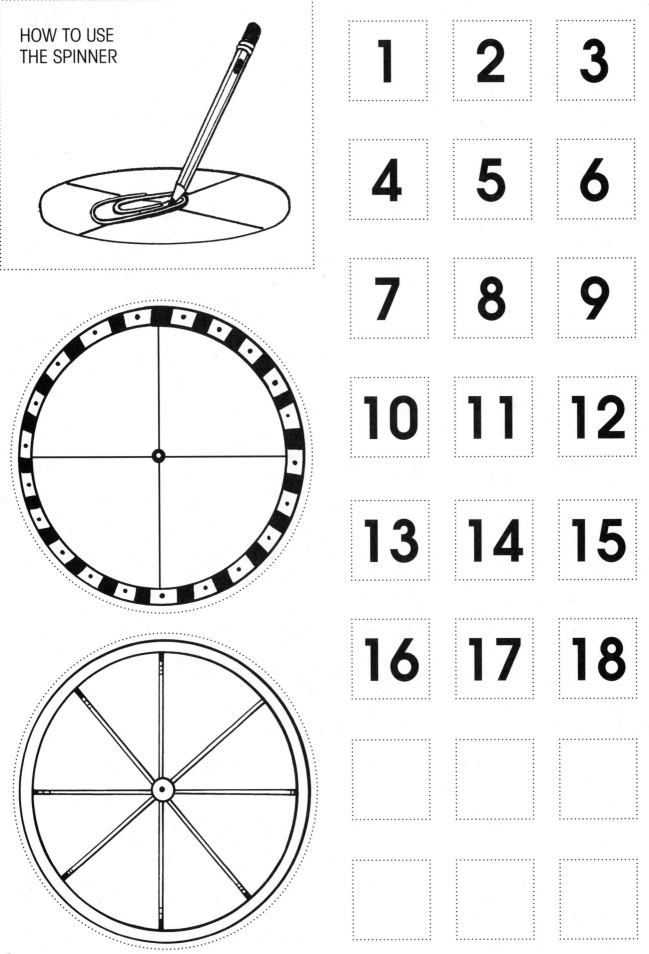

HOW TO USE
THE SPINNER

| 1 | 2 | 3 |
| 4 | 5 | 6 |
| 7 | 8 | 9 |
| 10 | 11 | 12 |
| 13 | 14 | 15 |
| 16 | 17 | 18 |

40

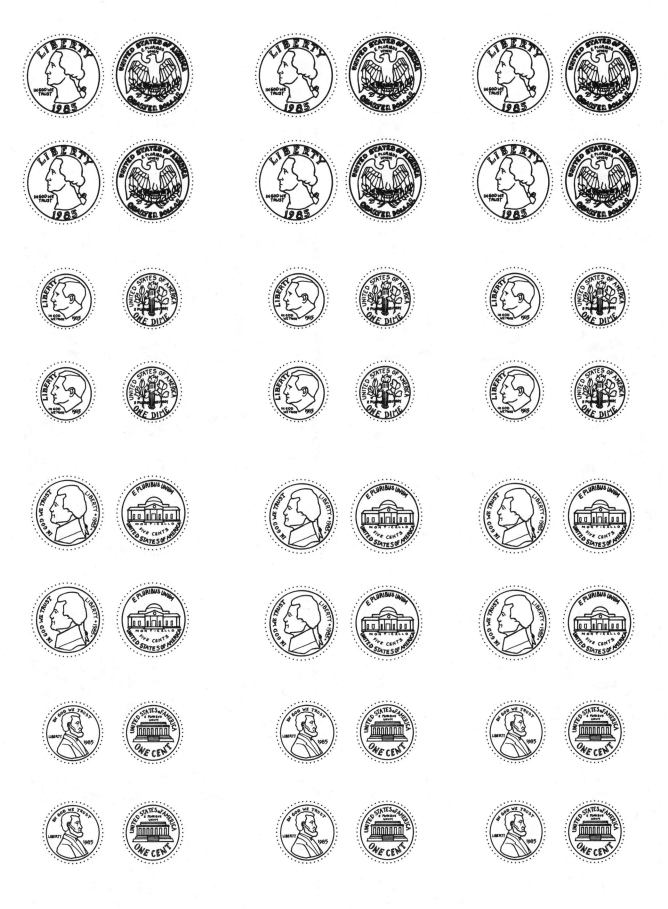

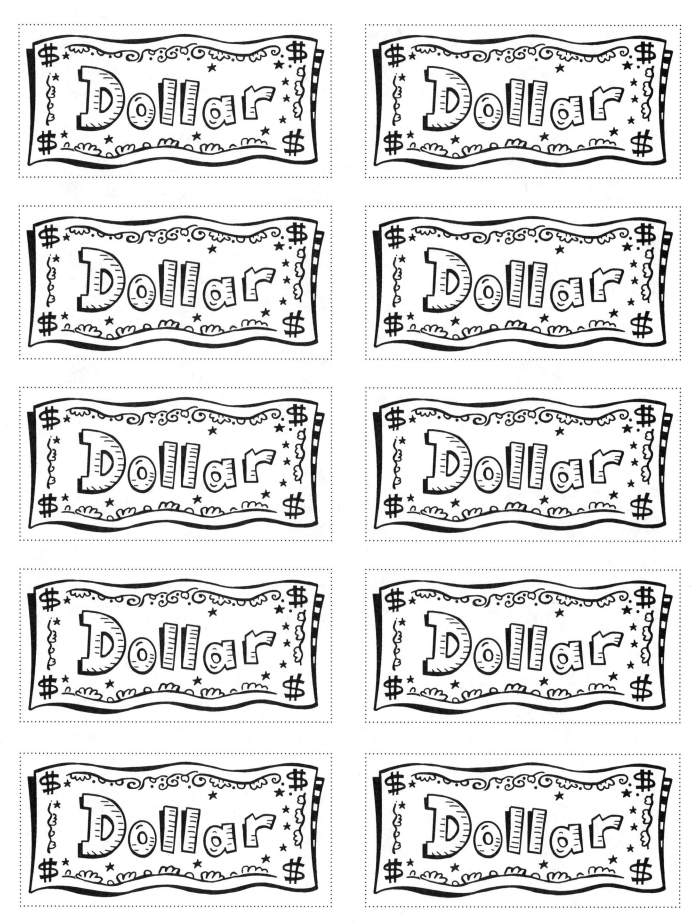

44

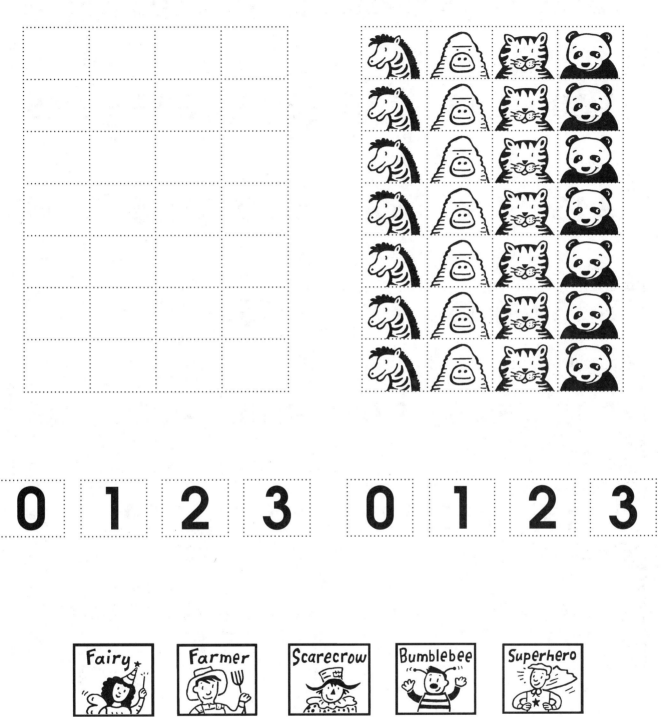

0 1 2 3   0 1 2 3

1 2 3 4 5

| | | | | | |
|---|---|---|---|---|---|
| 12:00 | 12:15 | 12:30 | 12:45 | 1:00 | 1:15 |
| 1:30 | 1:45 | 2:15 | 2:45 | 3:15 | 3:45 |
| 4:15 | 4:30 | 4:45 | 5:00 | 5:15 | 5:45 |
| 6:15 | 6:45 | 7:00 | 7:15 | 7:30 | 7:45 |
| 8:15 | 8:45 | 9:00 | 9:15 | 9:30 | 9:45 |
| 10:15 | 10:30 | 10:45 | 11:15 | 11:30 | 11:45 |

| | | | | |
|---|---|---|---|---|
| $\frac{1}{4}$ | $\frac{1}{2}$ | $\frac{3}{4}$ | $\frac{1}{3}$ | $\frac{2}{3}$ |

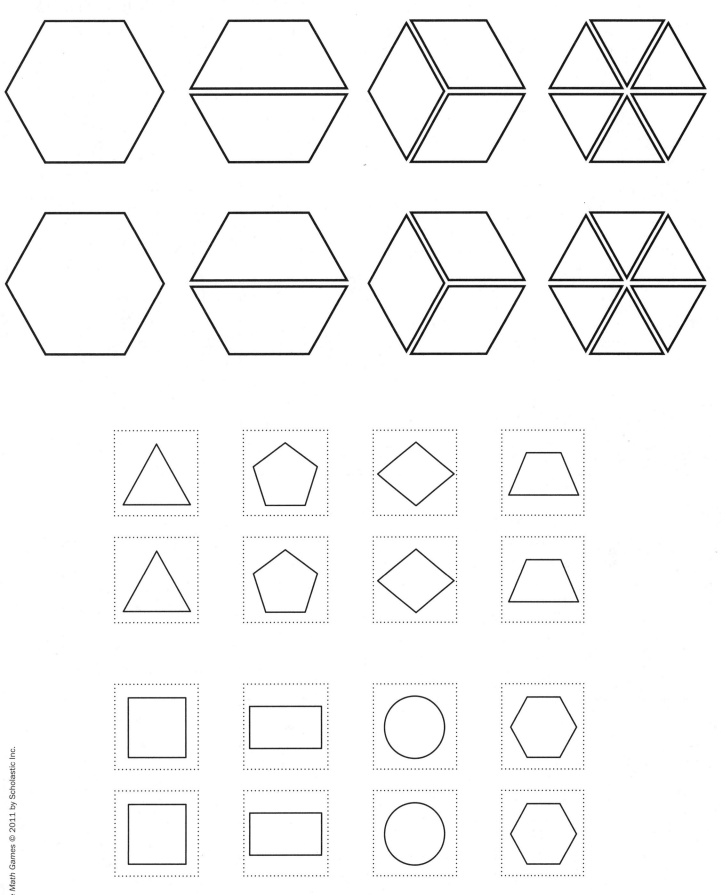

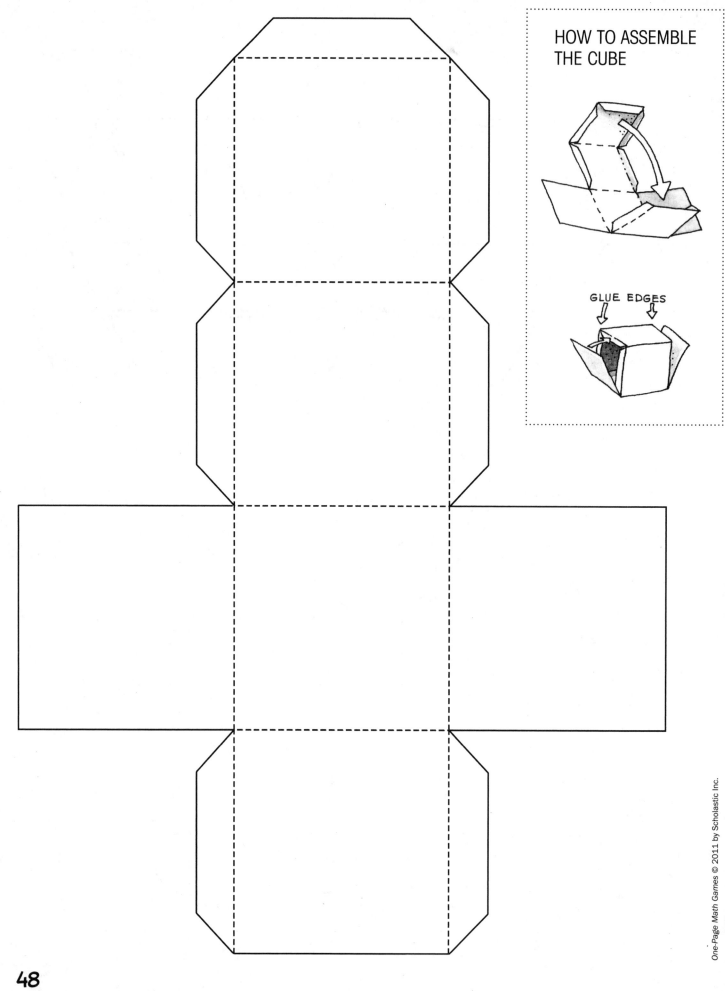

GLUE EDGES